FRENCH'S STANDARD DRAMA.

No. CLXVI.

FRANKLIN:

A NEW AND ORIGINAL

HISTORICAL DRAMA,

IN

FIVE ACTS.

BY JOHN BROUGHAM, COMEDIAN.

TO WHICH ARE ADDED,

A Description of the Costume—Cast of the Characters—Entrances and Exits—Relative Positions of the Performers on the Stage, and the whole of the Stage Business.

NEW-YORK:

SAMUEL FRENCH,

121 NASSAU-STREET.

Cast of the Characters.—(BENJAMIN FRANKLIN.)

Benjamin Franklin, (aged 17,)	Miss Kate Reignolds
Benjamin Franklin, (afterwards.)	Mr. Brougham.
Mr. Fishbourne,	Blake,
Mr. Keimar,	Barry,
Jasper Snook,	Hale,
Rory O'Fin,	Denham,
Rednose,	Brower,
William Pitt,	J. B. Howe,
Lord Hillsborough,	F. Hodges,
Lord Stormont,	Duncan,
Mr. Granite,	Bellamy,
Jabez,	Bilby,
Chevalier Papillotte,	M. Whiting,
Louis, King of France,	Flood,
Villeroi,	M. Post,
Honorable Mrs. Howe,	Miss Ingersoll,
Mrs. Keimar,	Miss F. Denham,
Mrs Franklin,	Mrs. Heald,
Mrs. Abiah Franklin,	Mrs. Axtelle,
Singing Bird,	Miss Pentington,
Pow Wow,	Miss McDonough,
Little Fox,	Miss Haywood.

Courtiers, Guards, Indians, Servants, &c.

STAGE DIRECTIONS.

EXITS AND ENTRANCES.

L. means *First Entrance, Left.* R. *First Entrance, Right.* S. E. L. *Second Entrance, Left.* S. E. R. *Second Entrance, Right.* U. E. L. *Upper Entrance, Left.* U. E. R. *Upper Entrance, Right.* C. *Centre.* L. C. *Left of Centre* R. C. *Right of Centre.* T. E. L. *Third Entrance, Left.* T. E. R. *Third Entrance, Right.* C. D. *Centre Door.* D. R. *Door Right.* D. L. *Door Left.* U. D. L. *Upper Door, Left.* U. D. R. *Upper Door, Right.*

*** *The Reader is supposed to be on the Stage, facing the Audience.*

Costumes.—(Franklin.)

FRANKLIN, (The Boy,)—Brown old-fashioned suit; gray stockings; three-cornered hat.

FRANKLIN—Second dress—Plain drab suit.

" Third dress—Gray suit, trimmed with fur; long white hair.

LOUIS—Light blue velvet coat, heavily embroidered; amber cuffs; blue breeches, stockings above the knees; long white satin vest, embroidered.

GENTLEMEN OF THE COURT—Similar dresses.

PAPPILLOTTE—Very elegant court suit; a muff.

FISHBOURNE,
KIEMAR, &c., &c., } —Dresses of the period.

WILLIAM PITT—Dark blue suit, embroidered.

LORD HILLSBOROUGH—Scarlet coat, embroidered; white vest and breeches.

LORD STORMONT—Dark embroidered suit.

SNOOK—First dress—light blue cutaway coat; tight pantaloons and short Hessian boots. Second dress—that of a "Beefeater."

O'FIN—First dress—a sailor's roundabout, dilapidated. Second dress—that of a wild Indian.

MRS. FRANKLIN—Dove-colored silk; white kerchief: hair in a roll.

MRS. ABIAH FRANKLIN—Dark dress of the period; gray hair.

MRS. HOWE—Handsome court suit.

LITTLE FOX,
POWWOW,
SINGING BIRD, } —Indian dresses.

FRANKLIN.

ACT I.

SCENE I.—*Market-street, in the Olden Time. Enter* KEIMER *and* WILLIAM FISHBOURNE, (R.)

Fish. Whither so fast, good master Keimer?

Keim Stay me not, worthy sir, for I am in much dole. I have lost, I may say, my right hand, the youth Rose—upon whom I trusted for the best part of my living. He died last night; and, in the very height of my sorrow, must I to my journal, endeavoring to do myself, what he was so worthy in. My neighbor Bradford will profit by my heavy loss.

Fish. Is there no other printer to be found?

Keim. Not one; there are but four in the whole city, of which Bradford has three, and I am left with but my own pair of hands to combat against his squad.

Fish. What hold you now, friend?

Keim. Within my mind, I hold an elegy to my poor friend and partner, Rose, which, for the lack of time, I shall compose in type. This is the astro sign of our good city, calculated by that famous astrologer, Jacob Taylor. It runs thus:—

"Full forty years have now their changes made,
Since the foundation of this town was laid;
When Jove and Saturn were in Leo joined,
They saw the survey of the place designed.
Swift were these planets, and the world will own,
Swift was the progress of the rising town.
A city built with such propitious rays
Will stand to see old walls and happy days."

Fish. 'Tis a good sign, worthy Master Keimer; pray Heaven it be prophetic.

Keim. Aye! that is a proper prayer for thee; and may I add, pray Heaven send me another printer. Farewell, good sir; if I find not aid, you may date my downfall from this heavy day [*Exit* KEIMER, L.

Fish. Poor Keimer! I lament his perplexity, notwithstanding his eccentric habits. Ah! what do I see? my old friend Nils, the Swede; one who remembers, not the first stone, but the first log driven in our youthful city.

(R.) *Enter* NILS GUSTAFSON, *aged* 70, *walking with staff.*

Fish. Let me assist you, worthy Nils.

Nils. Thanks, thanks, good sir; it is not long that I shall need mortal aid, nor do I wish it—seeing, as I do, this noble city, which, when a boy, I sported over. Ah! I remember well, here in this very street, laden with fine buildings, I had to cut my way through woods, to find a deer which I had shot. Nothing but one vast forest could be seen. The first load of wood, to build the first house, I helped to cut and carry.

Fish. Immortal honor to the name of Penn; he has just passed from amongst us, but his memory must live as long as time itself. 'Tis pleasing to render homage to those great men, who have preferred the interest of a remote posterity and times unknown to their own fortune and the quiet security of their own lives.

Nil. Ah! he was a great man. I well remember, about twenty years ago, when he left us to return to England, his last act was to make this a city. In half an hour you might have counted every house, and now look round.

Fish. Let thy mind carry thee still further, good Nils. If in its fortieth year we see such great results, what will a century bring forth? Methinks I see long lines of stately streets, a harbor crowded with the ships of every nation; where those few sheds are standing, a noble market place, filled with the choicest of provisions; a vast, busy multitude pursuing their respective bents of business or of pleasure. Famous in art, renowned for hospitality, my mind's eye takes in the whole. It must come, my worthy friend, for the elements of success are amongst us—industry, frugality, and perseverance.

Nil. Ah! would that I might live to look upon it; but 'tis blessing enough in one short life to see the foundation of a mighty empire laid.

Fish. Happy! thrice happy, they who will be born to see its full perfection; but come, let us no longer dream about the future; but that such future may be glorious, improve the passing time.

[*Exeunt* FISHBOURNE *and* NILS, L.

Enter YOUNG FRANKLIN, (*aged* 17,)—*sits on door step,* R.

Frank. And this is Philadelphia, the infant city I have read so much about. When I am a little rested, I must take a walk over it; it won't take me long, methinks. Well, here I am at the end of my journey, happy and independent. I have the mighty sum of one dollar in my pocket, which, with a slight knowledge of printing, a willing heart, and untiring industry, comprise my whole stock in trade. That long row in our boat has made me hungry: but where to get food I do not know. Had the man in the moon paid the earth a visit, he would probably find more acquaintance than I, for he might introduce himself to the spy-glass makers, but I, a poor, unknown and friendless wanderer, how shall I make friends?—why, the only way is by steadily pursuing an honest, straightforward, independent road, and proving myself worthy to be known. He who courts man's good opinion too sedulously, causes doubts of his own merits. The diamond doesn't covet to be seen, but, its value known, men covet it. So it is with friendship . the good attract the good, and I *mean* to be one amongst them. This is a gloomy commencement—poor, friendless and hungry, and might well dash down the thoughts of many, but I am not so easily dismayed ; energy is in my mind and hope in my heart, the petty ills of life I've early learnt to despise ; he who would rise, must climb at first ; if the child do not learn to creep, the man will have no power to run.—Pshaw ! if I stay moralising here, I'll lose my little strength for lack of sustenance. Did I but know where to find some bread—many a good meal I've made from that. [*Boy comes out of Shop in* F., *with Loaf and Exits*, L.] And lo at my very side, I find the means. Fortune, I thank thee ; and hail this as an augury of good. [*Enters Shop.*

Enter FISHBOURNE, L.

Fish. I foresee some trouble with this governor of ours ; he courts the public favor much too openly. Full of promises, which he has no intention to perform ; thoughtless and insincere, he may do much mischief. Whom have we here ?

Enter FRANKLIN, *with a Loaf under each arm.—He is eating.*

Fish. What are you about to do, my boy ?

Frank. [*Sitting on a Step*, R.] I am about to eat my dinner, sir, if you have no objection.

Fish Ha, ha ! independent, I see.

Frank. I have no reason to be otherwise, sir. This is not the bread of idleness—I have worked hard for it ; no one can claim a crust of it but me It is my own, sir, and I can eat it without a reproach.

Fish. It's a proud boast, my boy ; and I like it.

Frank. I'm glad you do, sir, for it shows you like what's right.

Fish. There's but little of the courtier about you, my lad.

Frank. If I thought flattery was needed, I wouldn't have come to Philadelphia.

Fish. You could not have paid our young city a nobler compliment, and I thank you for it. You interest me greatly,—and so, you are a stranger here ?

Frank. I hope not, sir

Fish. Why, I thought but now, you said you had just come ?

Frank. I grant it, sir : but I hope the honest and industrious heart will never be a *stranger* in an American city.

Fish. [*Aside.*] This is no common youth.—May I inquire what your profession is, my friend ?

Frank. A printer, sir ; and a poor one, as yet.

Fish. You must have had a superior education, for your choice of words, although rather bold are singularly apposite

Frank. I have, sir, received the best education in the world, in the school of adversity ; what little I know, I have taught myself, and one's self being the person likely to be most benefited, makes the best tutor.

Fish And your school was——

Frank. A tallow-chandler's shop, where I soon got a practical knowledge of early Greece, dipped into literature, and moulded a set of opinions for the regulation of my future conduct.

Fish. You astonish me!

Frank. It's nevertheless true, sir. My father was a poor tallow-chandler, with sixteen children, and I, the youngest of all, you may readily suppose he couldn't afford to pay much for our tutoring.

Fish. Have you, then, made yourself acquainted with the dead languages?

Frank. No, sir, I thought it better to improve my time by obtaining the *sense* of a living language, than to waste it in discovering the sounds of dead ones. My own language contains more ideas than I shall ever be able to acquire.

Fish. Such sound sense and plain reason in one so young, must shadow forth a manhood of no ordinary capacity. Who knows but in this poor, wayworn, unfriended boy, save by the mighty resources of his own intelligent mind, I may behold one whose after wisdom will sway the destinies of future ages, and whose name, now unknown, may shine, a bright particular star. I am not wrong, my lad, in supposing you to be an American?

Frank. It has been my fortunate lot to be so born, sir, and my only ambition is to be worthy of the name. My country and myself are both young; we shall grow together, and I confess I should like to do something that, in after time, may cause me to be, now and then, remembered with it.

Fish. And your name is——

Frank. Nothing when spoken by myself—when patriots and men of learning utter it, then and not till then, will I pride myself upon the name of—Benjamin Franklin.

Fish. Your frankness charms me; 'tis seldom that we hear the soul's secrets thus told without equivocation.

Frank. I have not learnt as far as equivocation, sir, and 'tis troublesome to *lie*.

Fish. Give me your hand—you are a noble boy. One friend you have for ever;—you must come home and dine with me.

Frank. Pardon me, sir, I feel grateful for your kindness. You saw me eat, and time is too precious for me to waste it in seeing you do the same. I must to business.

Fish. And that is?

Frank. To find a printer.

Fish. You need not look long. Fortune has paved the way for you,—the printer, Keimer, has just lost his best hand by death; you can step into his shoes.

Frank. They may not fit me;—but I'll wear them until I find a pair that will.

Fish. Come, I'll introduce you.—Stay: I suppose you are not too well off for funds; let me advance you some——

Frank. Sir, you said you would be my friend, and yet would you take from me that, without which none can be respected or respect himself—*Independence!* I am not blind, or lame, or idiotic; thank Heaven I have a mind to think with, and an arm well used to work,—

why, then, should I take that which I can procure myself? were sickness to fall on me, or accident, then would I gratefully accept thy loan; but while my health and strength remain, with my *own hands* will I assist destiny in shaping out my fate. I have discovered, even in my short experience, sir, that

> There is no want beneath the sky,
> That industry cannot supply.

[*Exeunt* FRANKLIN *and* FISHBOURNE, L.

SCENE II.—KEIMER'S *Printing Office and Drawing Room*—*he discovered at press, composing*—MRS. KEIMER, *on low seat, washing child, &c.*—*Uproar between mother and child.*

Mrs. K. (L. C.) Be quiet, will you! you cross-grained brat, let me wash you.

Keim. His corpse attended was by friends so soon——

[*Child cries.*]

His corpse——Will you keep that child still?

Mrs. K. I suppose you'll allow me to wash his face! But it's just like you men. I do believe you'd let the child run about with an inch of dirt growing on his dear face. Have done, do; you're always a bellowing!

Keim. [*Composing.*] From seven at morn till one o'clock at noon.

Mrs. K. Indeed it's no such thing. What do you mean by telling falsehoods about your own child. I wonder you're not afraid the roof will tumble in upon your unnatural head.

Keim. Woman, what are you talking about—don't you see I'm composing?

Mrs. K. Composing! A great deal of good that does. What are you composing now, I should like to know? eh!

Keim. An elegy on my poor friend Rose.

Mrs. K. I thought it was some stuff of that kind. You'd better do something useful. Think of your poor wife.

Keim. "By master printers carried to the grave."

Mrs. K. What? Oh! he's composing, I suppose. I only wish I was——

Keim. "Carried to the grave."

Mrs K. Flesh and blood cannot stand such aggravation. What do you mean by that? [*Rushes up to him.*

Keim. What's the matter now?

Mrs. K. Didn't I hear you say you wished I was carried to the grave?

Keim. You didn't hear anything of the kind. [*Child cries.*] Now do attend to that squalling epitome of yourself, and let me alone. Either keep your tongue still or come and compose yourself.

Mrs. K. Compose yourself. I'm sure you give yourself airs enough, if that's the same thing. [*Combs child's hair and makes his toilet.*] If you keep on writing nonsensical rhyming stuff, I should like to know where the money is to come from to keep house with.

Keim. "Nor failed our treasurer, in respect, to come."

Mrs. K. I see what will be the end of it; we shall want bread · I know we shall.

Keim. "Nor stayed the keeper of the rolls at home."

Mrs. K. What! you will aggravate me every minute. I can't say a word but you have some insulting reply. Now don't tell me you're printing that rubbish.' I know better; you're doing it on purpose, to break my spirit. I'm sure I'm one of the best creatures in the world, or I wouldn't be here, slaving for your comfort, in the way I do—when everybody knows I brought you a fortune of a hundred pounds; but it's like the ingratitude of man. I will speak! You think because I never raise my voice, that I'll sit down and endure every kind of conduct; but you're mistaken, sir.

[*She shoves the boy about in her impetuosity—he bellows.*

Keim. Oh! patience, patience! Will you let the child alone?

Mrs K. Who's touching him, I should like to know? It's your devilish temper that he inherits; and if I don't box it out of him, he'll come to be hanged, that's what he will—I'm sure I hope so.

Keim. For the love of Heaven, one moment's peace, 'till I finish this.

Mrs. K. Well, who's speaking? You're making all the fuss yourself. If you hadn't interfered, the child would have been dressed long ago.

Keim. "With merchants, shopkeepers, the young and old."

Mrs. K. To hear you speak, one would think I was a savage! I have my faults, I know——

Keim. "A numerous throng, not very easy told."

Mrs. K. Indeed! I suppose you'll tell me that's not insulting, but I'll let you know, there's a limit to everything—you good-for-nothing —— [*Going passionately up, meets*

FISHBOURNE *and* FRANKLIN, D. F.

Law, bless me, I'm sure, I beg your pardon, sir,—those servants, they do try one's temper. [*Aside to* KEIMER.] This is your fault, but I'll pay you off for it. Come along, Sammy, make a nice bow to the gentleman. [*Exit* MRS. KEIMER *and* CHILD.—FRANKLIN *down,* L. H.

Keim. [R.] I'm glad you came in, Mr. Fishbourne, or I think this might have stood for my own elegy—"troubles come thick upon my unfortunate head." Here's the governor's treaty with the Indian Chiefs to print, and as many as twelve advertisements; we're getting a great place—and only this one pair of hands to do it all.

Fish. [L. C.] I hope to relieve you somewhat, Master Keimer, and to that end have brought with me a printer.

Keim. Ha! ha! a printer! What, this boy a printer?

[FRANKLIN *dashes down his hat, rushes to the case, and rapidly selects type*—KEIMER *looking on amazed—strikes off impression.*

Keim. [C] Why, he *is* a printer, and, moreover, a most expeditious one. Why did you not say so?

Frank. (R.) The proof, sir, is better than the assertion. Economy is good, sir, even in time; and the greatest waste of time, is wasting words.

Keim. Bravo! bravo! This is not a human being, Mr. Fishbourne, --this is a guardian angel come to visit me in my extremity. I'll engage you as long as you please, on your own terms. I'll make a man of you yet, my lad.

Frank. I hope I shan't give you the trouble, sir.

Keim. Happy hour! I'm a new individual. There's your case: mark me, and your press;—never shall it be called so by any other. I needn't tell you what to do, for I see you have more sense in that young head, than half a dozen old ones.

Fish. [*Crosses to* C.] Farewell, my brave boy; it would be presumptuous in me to offer you one word of advice—only this, remember, that, should you ever need a friend, you'll find a staunch one in William Fishbourne.

Frank. Thank you, sir, thank you,—a noble heart like yours must know the feeling that now swells in mine.

Fish. It does, it does, my fine fellow; go on as you have begun, and your name will be remembered when ours are smothered in the dust of centuries. [*Exit* KEIMER *and* FISHBOURNE, C. D.

[*When they are off,* FRANKLIN *sinks on his knees and buries his face in his hands.*

END OF ACT I.

ACT II.

SCENE I.—*A Wood.*

Enter JASPER SNOOK, *a Londoner, and* RORY FIN, *an Irish Sailor,* L.

Fin. [*Sings.*] "I'll go no more a rovin', but constant as the dove."

Snook. Don't go for to make sich a hullabulloo, you noisy Irish sea-calf; how do you know what savages there may be at our very helbows?

Fin. Your soul to glory! don't you think I know the latitude I'm steerin' in, bad luck to your carrotty skull; ain't we right in the very thick of the savagest set of savages, that ever intruded a tomahawk into the brain of a Christian?

Snook. Don't say that, Mr Fin, if you don't want to see me dissolve away hinto a regular jelly. Oh! why did I come fortune-hunting into these wild, outlandish places? Ugh! what's that?

Fin. It's only a bear, you frightened donkey.

Snook. A what?

Fin. A bear! making his way through the bushes. If I had a gun here, I'd have a crack at him.

Snook. Here; I always carry firearms. Kill him, there's a good chap [*Gives very small pistol.*

Fin. Is it with this? Why this wouldn't knock a hole in a reasonable sized flea; don't be frightened, he ain't hungry.

Snook. Where *is* this Philadelphia? I wants to be in a place where there's brick walls, once more.

Fin. Why, then, you'll have to walk a mighty long distance, for all the brick houses here is built of wood.

Snook. My gracious! then the cargo of trowels and hods that I brought out.

Fin Will do to plaster up your courage—the devil a haporth else.

Snook. And the weavers' looms.

Fin Will make fine heir looms in your family. What else did you bring over?

Snook A lot of warming pans. They'll be nice in winter.

Fin. We must first get beds. Never mind, they'll make elegant mud scoopers. Well!

Snook, A most beautiful set of saddles and bridles.

Fin. That's elegant, provided they'll fit the cows and pigs. Them's the only beasts here at present.

Snook. Well, never mind—faint heart, you knows. Maybe I may meet some beautiful Indian princess like Miss Pocahontas, who will take a fancy to me. Wouldn't that be a go, eh? and I make my fortune!

Fin. How so?

Snook. Why, by taking her over to Lonnon, and showing her about for a shilling a head. There would be a spec! The savager the better! with a mouth like a saw-pit, rings in her nose, and fish-bones stuck in her ears. But come, let us be moving; it's getting dusky, and I can't say that I'm over-anxious to see any of the haboriginals. [*Going, suddenly finds an Indian standing beside him—moves off in the other direction—is intercepted by another*.] Oh! law; my blessed wig! I'm a corpse already; my last hour is come. Mercy! good-looking savage—mercy!

Enter TEAHOOK.

Tea. (R.) Stand up, what do you fear?

Snook. They're friendly haboriginals. Aye, stand up, white man, you have nothing to fear. Will you take a pinch of snuff? You don't happen to want any warming-pans?

Fin. Get out with your blackguard snuff; here's some elegant whiskey. Taste that, your majesty.

[REDNOSE, (L.) *is about to drink, when* TEAHOOK *dashes down flask*.

Tea. May the dark spirit keep in torture the soul that first found this destroying fire! Withered be the hand which offers it to the red man.

Fin. With all my heart, your wild reverence; there'll be more left for them that likes it. Here's your good health, any way.

Red. (L.) Give! [*Drinks stealthily*.

Fin. The devil take your swallow! Why the feller hasn't left as much as would suckle a butterfly's babby.

Tea. The red children of the forest journey to meet their white brethren, in the place of houses, to bid them welcome to our grounds. There is room enough for all. Leave us but the river to fish in, and the woods to hunt—and the pleasant valleys, which the white man loves, shall be his home, untouched and sacred.

Snook. Give us your fist; I like you. You are what I call a regular brick! You don't want any warming pans?

Red. [*Takes flask—tries*.] No more!! Ha! where is thy pleasant drink? Give—or—— [*Threatens*.

Fin. Is that your gratitude, you red vagabond? I've a great mind to measure your head for a new wig.

Tea. Stay, brother. The white man comes in friendship; let not our hands be the first to break the bond.

Red. [*Crosses* (C.) *to Snook.*] You have—eh—good drink for Indian? Give.

Snook. Take him off! I've none, I say.

Red. Give! [*Seizes snuff-box, puts to mouth, sneezes and makes faces.*] Great Spirit! you punish poor Indian. Oh! great, great——

[*Kneels, and paws* SNOOK.

Snook. We forgive you; but don't be so familiar, red individual.

Red. Rednose stay with great whites. One good—give fine drink! other bad—give tickle dirt for nose. Ah! make sneezy. Whiskey grand!—warm his heart—make eyes dance, and legs shake about, fine; Ha, ha! me drink like big fish—but no more tickle dirt!

Tea. Brother, you have closed the place of sense, drowned your brains in bad drink—ah! I foresee more destruction to the red man from that dreadful scourge than from all the arrows of the enemy. Retire, you are not fit to be amongst warriors; you are conquered by a child, beaten by water, go! [*Exit* TEAHOOK.

Red. Me hab dance first, fire water good enemy, take brains away, but leave scalp; good enemy, me like him, hi! hi! [*Dances.*

Fin. Never be it said that a gentleman couldn't go down a jig for want of a partner. Come along, old yallow ochre.

[*They dance and drag* SNOOK *about—Exeunt.*

SCENE II.—FRANKLIN'S *Apartment.*

MRS. FRANKLIN, L., *and* MR. FISHBOURNE, R., *discovered.*

Mrs. F. Providence has indeed blessed us largely, Mr. Fishbourne; but me, most particularly, in giving me so great, so good a man, to be my husband.

Mr. Fish. My dear Mrs. Franklin, great as he has become amongst us, 'tis, I'm confident, but the imperfect shadow of his approaching glory that we contemplate: nearly twenty years he has lived here, and, he has won the esteem of all, by his affability, and their wonder by his philosophic attainments. From the man who, self taught and self directed, even now compels the lightning from the skies, what may we not anticipate? Borne upward through the elements of science by the innate force of his own energy, the long cherished fallacies of ages he crumbles with a touch, the mighty strength of his unerring judgment battering down the strongholds of falsehood, not for himself alone, but to benefit a universe.

FRANKLIN *without,* L. H.

Frank. Time is money, friend, time is money, don't waste it; good day.—Come *you* in, friend, I'll speak to thee, as I [*Enters with* WILKINS, L. H.] Ah! my good [*Crosses to* C.] Fishbourne, your servant,—wife, yours, [*Takes off wig and great coat as he speaks, which* MRS. F. *hangs up,*] now, friend, speak, how can I serve thee?

Wilk. Honored sir——

Frank. Stop! I must pay my respects to his honor, [*Looks round,*] where is he? who were you speaking to?

Wilk. To *you*, worthy sir.

Frank. I admit the worth, at least, I try to make myself so: but go on, flattery tickles not my ear; what do you want?

Wilk. I have heard, sir, of your universal goodness.

Frank. Then you've heard a lie, and I'll trouble you not to add another to it—Eh! wife, you recollect our scheme, to attain absolute perfection; presumptuous fools that we were! Divine wisdom gave us a wholesome admixture of passions, and we wanted to pick out all the plums: but this is gabble. Go on, friend, I can mend my pens the while, it requires no thinking, and I can't get on unless either my head or my hands are at work.

Wilk. Indeed, sir, I am ashamed to say what I have come for.

Frank. Did you come to lie or to steal?

Wilk. No, sir!

Frank. Then you ought to be ashamed of yourself for being ashamed. What then induced you to come?

Wilk. My great poverty.

Frank. That's a matter easily remedied; honesty, industry, and independence, compose a capital that will soon open an account. Have you these?

Wilk. I fear me I have not, sir, to a sufficient——

Frank. There, sir, I know you *have*—what are you?

Wilk. Nothing but a mechanic, sir.

Frank And pray, sir, what *can* you *be* better? Learn to estimate yourself at your own worth, and others will soon follow the example; brother mechanic, give me your hand! The world has too long been humbugged—aye, humbugged—by these invidious distinctions between man and man, but this pretty porcelain of humanity is getting brittle from age, and should it come in contact with the hardy potter's clay, it would come second best out of the conflict. You have a trade, and cannot get employment—is it not so?

Wilk. It is, sir.

Frank. What a saving of time it would have been, had you said so at first. Wife, give me a few more quills. Now listen to me, sir, I am going to lend you some money,—I never give,—I'm not rich enough for that. Here, sir, are forty pounds.

Wilk. [*Starting.*] No, sir! I ——

Frank. I say, yes, sir. Don't interrupt me; will that be enough to set yourself up in your trade?

Wilk. Bless you, sir, more than enough. Bless you, for this act of charity.

Frank. Don't talk nonsense; it's a matter of business. You must repay me, and without fail.

Wilk. I shall, sir, if I live and keep my strength. At what time?

Frank. When you see an honest man struggling in the toil of poverty, pay *him* that forty pounds, enjoining the same terms on him—so that before it reaches the hand of a rascal, I hope it may bring comfort to the hearts and homes of hundreds.

Wilk. Accursed be the hand that stays so benevolent a plan. With tears of gratitude I thank you.

Frank. Stuff—stuff; be a man,—perform your contract, therein will lie my best recompense; but my pens are all mended, I must bid you good bye.

Wilk. Heaven bless and prosper you. [*Exit*, L. H.

Frank. Thank you, thank you. [*Goes to Desk—Writes: speaking the while.*] Well, my kind old friend, our obstinate council has consented at last to my plan f r a general militia. Wife, you will have an opportunity of witnessing a vast military display shortly; the peaceful streets of Philadelphia, fo: the first time, will echo to the martial tread of a citizen soldiery. I am glad that I have carried my plan, for in time of danger, either from riot at home, or threatened invasion from abroad, who can best protect our hearts and homes, than those to whom they are most near and dear?

Fish. Does your far-seeing eye apprehend danger from abroad?

Frank. [C] I sometimes think that the day is not far distant when we shall need our coolest heads, our stoutest hearts; our country approaches its maturity The rod which awes and subjugates the *youth*, must not be laid upon the back of *manhood*.

Fish. And think you *that* will be the policy of our rulers?

Frank. It *may* be;—if it *should*, their rule is limited—the plant will soon become a tree, whose leaves must be *freedom* and whose fruit, *independence*.

Fish. It glads me much to hear those sentiments from you, for I have dared to think that we were not ordained to live for ever in dependence.

Mrs. F. [L.] You make me feel much anxiety, Mr. Fishbourne. Kind heaven avert a civil warfare.

Frank. Wife, be quiet; no speech of ours can stay the march of destiny; it is ordained that this, our vast, but thinly populated country is to become a mighty nation.—I can see its future glory, trace its onward progress, step by step,—like a man of business, I look at it with a business eye. Were they to make us equal partners, we might get on together for a while, but to keep us in an eternal apprenticeship is beyond all natural indenture.

Fish And what think you will be the result?

Frank. Why we'll have to set up for ourselves; that's all. But, wife, by-the-bye, have you given orders to get my travelling trunk stocked? You know I am off to see my good old mother· 'tis now some twenty years since we have met; I have two reasons for this visit—the first, to pay a debt of filial duty; the next, to prove the truth or fallacy of that natural instinct philosophers speak of; I am so much changed, 'twill be *instinct* alone will cause her to recognize me.

Mrs. F. All is prepared.

Frank. Let's to dinner, then,—come, Fishbourne. Of the changes which may,—nay, *must* come, *think* much but speak little. Perilous times require prudent tongues.

END OF ACT II.

ACT III.

SCENE I.—*An Indian Encampment.*

(L. H.) *Enter* O'FIN *and* SNOOK, *partly dressed like Indians.*

Fin. Well, my cockney friend, how do you like your Indian Chief sort of life? Ain't you an elegant specimen of aristocracy?

Snook. Yes, I dare say. I only wish I could get away from this, anyhow. I'm tired of being a Hindian.

Fin. Why? ain't you happy in your power, and your multiplication of Mrs. Snookes?

Snook. That's it. The polybigamy is dreadful! One woman's tongue is bad enough, to be always chiming in one's ears; but to have a trio of squaws squalling eternally ain't the cheese, no how.

Fin. Haven't I done my endeavors to alleviate your connubial misery? Havn't I made love to them in elegant Irish? But they are so infatuated with you, all my blandishments and blarney makes no more effect than if they were my wives instead of yours.

Snook. Poor unhappy me. When the Hindians offered to take me with them, and to ornament my good looking countenance in this outlandish way, I thought I was a going to be a reglar Julius Cæsar. I wish I wasn't so hawful fascinating. If I was only tolerable good-looking, these devils of Hindian women wouldn't keep on marrying me in such a extravagant way. But why don't you go into the marrying line?

Fin. Is it me? By my soul, there's only one creature that lives in my heart; and there she'll stick as long as there's any heart's blood left to warm her.

Snook. How awful romantic—and who mought she be?

Fin. Never you mind; that's my secret. [RED NOSE *sings without,* (L.)—"*Wine cure da gout, da colums and da tizz*"] Hallo! Here comes our respectable friend, Mr. Red Nose—our pupil, whom we are endeavoring to civilize.

Snook. Well, and ain't he getting on like a brick?

Fin. Yes, as far as smoking and drinking goes he's about as civilized as any dandy that walks Bond-street.

Snook. Ah! poor old Bond-street. When will we ever see you again? Never—I'm afraid, never.

Fin. Pshaw! Man, never despair. What the devil does it signify, where a fellow eats and drinks, so as he has enough of that same, anyhow? Here comes a savage genius, that has had a thrifle too much of the latter condiment.

Enter RED NOSE, *half-civilized in dress, a big wig, pipe, &c., singing "Wine cures da gout."*

Red. Ha! me glad to see. Got wig—me gentleman, now—mo lord.

Fin. Yes, you're as drunk as one.

Snook. You've been at that wine again, Mr. Red.

Red. No, whisk—physic for Indian—make forget all kicks.

Fin. Oh! you're a fine article for summer wear. But come, it's time for you to say your lesson.

Red. Me ready—little drop fuss—make remember.
Snook. Now, spell—spell squaw !
Red. Don't want spell him.
Snook. Say *her*, fool.
Red. Her fool—dat you—me know dat. Ha ! ha !
Fin. You're an apt scholar. We'll make something of you yet. Now, spell good.
Red. G-u-d.
Fin. Very good boy. Now what does good mean ?
Red. Me know dat like book. Good mean rum !
Fin. How can that be ? Isn't there bad rum as well as good ?
Red. No. No bad rum. *Better* rum, but no bad.
Fin. When are you going to let us dance at your wedding, Mr. Red Nose ?
Red. When me find squaw with no mouth.
Red. Why no mouth ?
Red. Dere isn't rum enough for two.
Fin. You're a selfish ould vagabond. [*Crosses to* C.] Dare we trust him with our intention of making our way to Philadelphia ?
Snook. (R.) If we take him with us, we'll be obliged to have a pack-horse to carry the whiskey he'll drink.
Fin. (C.) Let us pump him. Red, do you remember Philadelphia ?
Red. Oh ! yes. Phillydel—grand, big drunk there. Such squaw ! Such whisk ! Oh !
Fin. Would you like to go there again ?
Red. Not care. Wherever dere's whisk, no sorrow—no wisk, all black—plenty whisk, all sun.
Snook. Do you think you could guide us there ?
Red. Easy as to drink. What for you want to go ?
Fin. He's tired of authority, and wants to repose on his laurels—to sit at home all day, and keep on mixing whiskey punch for you and me to drink. Eh !—my Bacchus of the wilderness—how would you like that ?
Red. Big—great big, like—let us go.
Snook. Stop—not yet. We must collect some eatables, or we should starve.
Red. Ha, ha ! rifle stop dat. Dry wood—powder—big fire—nice roasty—big drink—good. Oh ! me see, you wait for all squaw. Like much tongue, talky talk—make head whiz. [*Women's voices.*
Snook. Hush ! Not a word.
[*A great chattering heard,* R. H.—SNOOK *starts off,* L.

Enter SINGING BIRD, LITTLE FOX, *and* POW WOW, *after* SNOOK.

Red. Too much squaw ! [*Exit opposite,* L.

(L.) *Re-enter* SQUAWS, *with* SNOOK.

Fin. Now, for a touch of the domestic.
Fox. You no bring Little Fox nice bead. } *All together.*
Pow. Nor Pow Wow—me angry, very. }
Bird. What you brought me ? }

Snook. One at a time, wives of my bosom. Squaws of my affection, I have only two ears.

Fin. And a squaw too much even for them. Well, I won't intrude on your trio of connubiality. [*Exit.*

Snook. How the devil shall I get rid of these turtles? My beloved helpmates, I and my friend are going to fish to catch something for dinner.

Pow. Me go too—me never leave de lovely Snook—her husband.

Fox. Me, too—me stick fast as de branch to de tree.

Bird. And me, hang round him neck like nice beads round de neck of Singing Bird.

Snook. Oh, this is too much felicity! What a terrible thing it is to be a fascinating individual in a thinly populated country. Spouses, listen to your lord and master——

Pow. Me listen much.

Bird. Me drink in words.

Fox. Me, too. So I——

Snook. I must exercise the authority of a husband. What the devil do you want?

Pow. Me jealousy.

Bird. And me—oh, very!

Fox. So me—all jealousy. [*They pursue him round the stage.*] Could kill—one little stick kill jealousy dead.

Snook. Yes, and kill me too. Diabolical squaws, what's the matter now?

Fox. Me saw you look—look—out of your beautiful eyes at strange squaw.

Pow. Me, too! Take care, me tear eyes out. [*Business and exit.*

SCENE II.—*Boston.—Interior of a plain, substantial chamber, old-fashioned.*—MRS. ABIAH FRANKLIN (*about* 60), *discovered knitting.—Several persons round fire.*

Gran. Cold night this, Mrs. Franklin.

Mrs. F. It is indeed, Mr. Granite. God help the poor creatures who have scant covering in those perishing times. Here, Jabez, put another log on. [*Enter* JABEZ *with log,* L.] That's too large—enough, but no waste.

Gran. Right, Mrs. Franklin. By the bye, your son is making a great figure in the world, I hear.

Mrs. F He is, and he deserves it: 'tis long since I have seen him, although I hear from him nearly every mail. Plagued and harassed though he is with public business, still he never neglects his duty and his love to me.

Gran. Then he must succeed. Hark, how the wind blows—a terrible night for the seamen.

Enter JABEZ *with log.*

Mrs. F. That's right; wilful waste makes woful want, Jabez. Save a little from your own store, and give to those who want it more. Remember that, Jabez. [*Exit* JABEZ.—*Knocks at* L. *door.*] Come in.

Enter FRANKLIN *in great coat.*

Frank. Good day, Madam. Gentlemen, your servant. Here, boy, [*Enter* JABEZ, R.] take my coat and hat—be very careful of my wig-box—it's my Sunday one—do you hear? Before I go any further, as I am a strange gentleman, I wish to say a word or two to you all. [*All turn round curiously.*] As I understand you have considerable curiosity about strangers, I will just at once give you a brief history of myself. I am a printer by trade, just turned of forty years old, come here to see some friends and collect some debts. I have a wife and two children; they both go to school, and have had the measles. I ride my own horse and have paid for the saddle: I am exactly five feet eight inches in height, and don't owe anything to my tailor. [*All resume places.*] Egad, there don't seem to be much chance of my thawing my toes at that fire! Here, boy, [*Enter* JABEZ] go and give my horse a peck of oysters. [*All turn round.*

Job. Oysters, sir!

Frank. In the shell—my horse never eats them any other way.

[*Exit* JABEZ, L.—*all rush out after.*—FRANKLIN *quietly sits down.*—MRS. F. *having put by her knitting, puts on caleche and is going.*

—My dear madam, don't trouble yourself; it was but a trick of mine to get near your cheerful fire.

Mrs. F. I think, sir, you took a great liberty, whoever you are, to send my friends into the cold.

Frank. I thought they kept me in it long enough—you have some rooms here, have you not, for travellers?

Mrs. F. No, sir! We can't take nobody knows who into the house.

Frank. Oh! very well! Nature, instinct!—humbug! [*Aside.*] It's a cold night, but never mind, there's something even worse than that to be endured.

Mrs. F. Put that coat down, do you think I'm a savage? You can stay the night.

Frank. Dear old soul, I knew it; now could I hug her, but I'll give nature another chance. Well, my good lady, and how do you get on here, eh?

Mrs. F. What's that to you? For one who rebuked *our* curiosity, you seem to have a tolerably fair share.

Do whate'er you teach,
Or don't attempt to preach,

my good man.

Frank. Fairly answered. May I make so free as to ask your name?

Mrs. F. *Franklin!*

Frank. Rather an uncommon one; yet, I think I've heard it before.

Mrs. F. Where do you come from?

Frank. Philadelphia.

Mrs. F. Indeed!—and you *think* you've heard the name of Franklin.

Frank. I'm almost sure I have.

Mrs. F. [*Rising in anger.*] It will be heard of, sir, where yours will never be whispered—it will live, sir, when yours is rotting in forgotten dust.

Frank. No, it won't!

Mrs. F. Do you know, sir, to whom you are speaking?

Frank. To a lady, I trust

Mrs. F To a woman, sir—to a mother!

Frank. Madam, I know it.

Mrs. F. Then, how dare you speak as you do?

Frank. I only say what I know, that this same Franklin, your son, is no better than he should be; no one knows that better than I do; he's a fool, and a——

Mrs. F. [*Seizing warming-pan.*] Leave my house, you insolent——

Frank. One moment, before I go—do you remember the last words that passed between you and Ben before he quitted for Philadelphia?—Your words were these: "Be honest, frugal, and industrious, and take a mother's blessing!" [*She drops warming-pan.*] And his to you were: "Let come what may, mother, I shall never forget thee."

Mrs. F. It is my Benjamin.

Frank. Mother! [*Embrace.*

Mrs. F. Oh! Ben, Ben, why did you do this?

Frank. To solve a problem, mother, and prove that there's no such thing as instinct. All humbug, nothing but humbug!—But it must be nearly supper time.

Mrs. F. Thou shalt have some—but bless thee, what a man thou 'rt grown!—I knew it—I knew it—my own Ben! [*Enter crowd,* L.

Gran. Sir, sir, I say, your horse won't take the oysters!

Frank. I didn't say he would; you 'd better bring them to me.

Gran. What!—don't he *eat* oysters?

Frank. Yes, sir, as often as I eat hay! 'Tis only when upon a cold evening I find every seat before the fire occupied, and not one move to give the stranger room, that I *show* my horse a peck of oysters, in order that those who keep me in the cold should taste a little of it themselves.

[*All look sheepish*—JABEZ *and* MRS. F. *laugh—Tableau*

END OF ACT III.

ACT IV.

SCENE I.—*Interior of a Show.*

RORY O'FIN, *as Indian, and* JASPER SNOOK *discovered, drinking and smoking pipes.—Very indifferent Band playing outside*

Snook Bad business this, Rory; my boy.

Fin. Won't pay for the music.

Snook. Music?

Fin. Excuse the remark; it's as good as most exterior orchestras. How much have we taken to-day?

Snook. Three shillings;—a shilling for the room, that must be paid; a shilling for the band, they won't blow a breath without it——

Fin. And sixpence apiece profit.

Snook. Walker!—you forget the engine.

Fin. What engine?

Snook. Why, the mighty engine, the press.

Fin. Murdher alive! then we hav'n't got a rap for ourselves.

Snook Don't be downcast—it's the fate of genius.

Fin. I know, I know Tear an' nouns, I didn't wonder at not being able to make the pot boil while I was in a legitimate way of business, but I did have some hope that when I condescended to become a humbug, I might bamboozle the public as well as the rest of them.

Snook. Patience; we'll do it still,—I havn't brought out my trump card, yet.

Fin. What is it?

Snook. You shall eat a babby.

Fin. Eat a what?

Snook. A babby.

Fin. Get out, you ruffian—I'll dissolve partnership.

Snook. Nonsense. We've given the multitude an opportunity to see a real live Indian, and, barring the brogue, you make a very good imitation; now I'll have to paint you as a cannibal—so that there's a terrible picture of the bloody repast blazing on the outside, it ain't much matter what we do within; we can tell the humane and judicious populace that you're not hungry, they're a little too late, or babbies is scarce; I tell you the only fault we have committed is, that we didn't go it strong enough.

"A little *humbug* is a dangerous thing," &c.

Hollo! what's that?

Fin. Hurrah! a shilling; I'll swear to the sound.

Snook. As I'm a live showman, here's a rush of two more. Well—get up, roar your ruffian, roar; get into the cage.

Fin. I'm too drunk!—I'll put my foot in it;—I know.

[*Becomes savage.*

Enter SEVERAL PEOPLE.

Snook. Don't go near him; he's wery dangerous.

[*He pokes at him with stick,*—FIN *roars.*

Visitor. What a terrible monster!

Lady Visitor. Frightful! Does it speak?

Snook. Like a good 'un, marm. Hollo, you, give this here lady a specimen of your noble tongue. [FIN *speaks in Irish.*

Visitor. What a singular language.

Snook. Yes, sir, it's a sort of cross between High Dutch and Low Grunt. [RORY *sings.*] Confound the fellow, the whiskey's playing the devil.

Lady Visitor. Why, he has quite a voice.

Fin. Voice—I believe I have.

Visitor. Hollo! there's a strong potatoe flavor about that.

Fin. What the devil have you got to say agin' the potatoes, eh ould spoonbill? Hurrah!

Potatoes grows in Limerick,
And beef in Ballimore;
The buttermilk is beautiful,
But that you knew before.

Hurrah for Kelamanaisy and the blue sky over it.

Lady. [*Screams*.] Ah ! the savage is breaking loose.

Fin. Get out, you murdhering lot of pippin squeezin ragamuffins.

[*General row*—MUSICIANS *rush in.*—SNOOK *is knocked into a drum*, *&c.*, *&c.*

SCENE II.—*Council Chamber in the Palace of St. James's.*

LORD STORMONT, MR. PITT, LORD HILLSBOROUGH.

Stor. (L.) I assert it, my lord ; the great director of disaffection in the colonies is this very philosopher Franklin, for whom you express so much interest.

Pitt. (C.) Sir, it is not in the power of one single man to convulse and overturn a mighty empire, no more than the chip which floats upon the surface of the wave, has power to lash it into fury. It is our own fault ; the obstinate stupidity of our own government, which brought about this momentous crisis ; as we sit with closed doors, I can say thus much without the imputation of treason.

Hills. (R.) Strange language for a minister, though.

Pitt. Sir, this is no time to varnish over circumstances ; it is impossible to give open injustice the semblance of right. I repeat it, we have done wrong, and I am glad the colonies have resisted.

Stor. (L.) Still, is it right that we should entrust so responsible a charge, as the head of the post office, to a man who may turn it to his own advantage—to one of the bitterest enemies this country ever knew.

Pitt My lord, my lord, recollect of whom you speak, a man who has obtained the reverence of Europe, who is an honor, not only to his place of birth, but to human nature.

Stor. He possesses your sympathy in an extraordinary degree, Mr. Pitt. You do him honor.

Pitt. Sir, I do him justice ; his honor springs from himself.

Hills. We had better examine him, and ascertain his exact sentiments, and then act accordingly. Parliament has granted us a discretionary power—shall it be so, Mr. Pitt?

Pitt. I am content ; but you may as well spare yourselves the pains ; you will get no admission from him.

Hills. Who waits there?

Enter LIVERY SERVANT, C. D.

Hills. Is Mr. Franklin in the antechamber?

Serv. He is, my lord.

Hills. Conduct him here.

Pitt. With respect! [*Exit* SERVANT, C. D.] My lords, recollect that you have to deal with no common man, but one, who, to the modest demeanor of Phocion, adds the wisdom and spirit of Socrates ; one who, to the fame of a philosopher and philanthropist, adds that of a statesman and patriot.

Enter two SERVANTS *in rich livery, followed by* FRANKLIN. SERVANTS *Exit.*

Pitt. Be seated. [*He sits* L. H.] Mr. Franklin, it will be necessary for us as commissioners appointed by Parliament, to question you; but be assured, as far as I am concerned, my respect for your character will oblige me, as it should all others, to use the greatest delicacy in this, to me unpleasant duty.

Frank. Sir, I thank you for your good opinion; but I pray you to use no delicacy in your questioning, as I shall certainly use none in my answers.

Stor. In the first place, do you think the colonies will pay this stamp duty?

Frank. No.

Pitt. Not if it be moderated?

Frank. Never! unless by force of arms.

Stor. How, if we stop the imports? what would you do for British manufactures?

Frank. Do without them—*we* have plenty of material, and plenty of industry, to make and wear our own.

Hills. We!—you take a decided stand by those malcontents.

Frank. Who *should* I stand by?

Stor. By your king!

Frank. I have a higher duty still than that.

Hills. And it is——?

Frank. To my country!

Stor. Of course; with such opinions as you entertain, you cannot expect to keep the lucrative position you occupy at present. We must dismiss you.

Frank. I have not waited for that, my lord. I came into this room a free agent, else would my tongue have been tied: I am no longer in the service of your government.

Hills. [*Rising.*] To what government, sir, *do* you owe obedience?

Pitt. [*Rising.*] My lord, you have no right to ask that question. Mr. Franklin is now a British subject. Should he not long remain so, you will only have yourselves to blame that so distinguished a man be lost to us. Mr. Franklin, will it please you to retire. [*Servants enter and go out with* FRANKLIN.—*All sit but* PITT, *who salutes cordially.*] My Lords, I must congratulate you upon your skilful diplomacy; you have changed a friend into an unconquerable foe.

Stor. We must temporize: he cannot be lost——

Pitt. 'Tis too late. What do you propose?

Hills. To entrap him into some admission of his treasonable designs—then have him denounced and punished.

Pitt. If this be your policy, I will have no act or part in it. My Lords, I leave you to your honorable intentions, with this assurance, that to the meanness of duplicity you will add the ignominy of defeat.

[*Exit* PITT, C.

Stor. Think you we can cage this cunning fox?

Hills. It will be a difficult matter. Stay: when men's judgment fail in accomplishing a desirable end, the tact of woman often succeeds. Let me see—whom can we employ in so delicate a matter? Ha, I have it: he's fond of chess, and Lord Howe's sister plays sufficiently. We'll bring them together. He will be here shortly by appointment,

It will be hard if our cunning and her wit be not a match for this subtle sage. The lightning of a woman's eye may probably dazzle his philosophy.

SCENE II.—*Splendid Apartment.*—MRS. HOWE *discovered.*—*Chess table-board.*—LORD STORMONT—LORD HILLSBOROUGH.

Stor. Think you that he will come?

Mrs. H. Certainly he will.

Stor. Then you know your lesson—draw him on by degrees; and could you but surprise him into an indiscreet avowal, it will be a game well played, and for a princely stake.

Mrs. H. But not to bring him personal danger. You must promise that, else I aid not in your plot.

Hills. That's easily done. My dear madame, we promise. We can't help it if it should turn out otherwise. [*Aside to* STORMONT.—*Servant announces*, Doctor Franklin, c.] The enemy approaches—courage!

[STORMONT *and* HILLSBOROUGH *retire.*

Mrs. H. Oh, I'm afraid. [*Enter* FRANKLIN.] My dear Mr. Franklin, good morning—pray be seated.

Frank. With pleasure, madam.

Mrs. H. You are partial to chess, I believe, Doctor,—are you not?

Frank. Exceedingly so, madam.

Mrs. H. Will you deem me not too presumptuous if I attempt a trial of skill with you?

Frank. 'Tis I who should apologize, madam.

Mrs H. [*To servant.*] Place the chess-board, Simpson. [*It is placed.*] Doctor, there's something to me wonderfully exciting in this game, as my mind gets interested: I could now fancy it a field of deadly strife, where in fierce contest rival armies deal destruction round; again, it brings before my vision scenes of crafty statesmanship, when wily courtiers vainly strive to fish out the minnow of truth from an ocean of falsehood. It's your move.

Frank. I know it. I did but deliberate.

Mrs. H. You are not attending to me.

Frank. Pardon me, madam. I see your move.

Mrs. H. Indeed!

Frank. In the game only—check to your king!

Mrs. H. Ah! you speak that with an air of triumph, doctor.

Frank. It's a triumphant position, lady.

Mrs. H. Sir!

Frank. On the chess-board, madam.

Mrs. H. You see he's out of danger, now.

Frank. He had to retire, though. See how perseverance makes small things of importance. This poor pawn, the lowest piece upon the board—without the aid of either knight or bishop—this base, rebellious, democratic pawn, has had the power to put a check on majesty.

Mrs. H. [*Insinuatingly.*] What would you infer from that, Doctor?

Frank. That chess is a very interesting game, madam.

Mrs. H. [*Taking pawn.*] Now, sir, where is your audacious pawn?

Frank. He's gone, but leaving behind him a rich legacy. Now you see the necessity of temper and caution. I take in exchange your castle; and by the same move check both king and knight.

Mrs. H. And by a miserable pawn again; how provoking. Doctor, you've pushed that pawn up most treasonably; but he shan't escape; I'll take him.

Frank. You can't, he's guarded by a brother pawn.

Mrs. H. So it is. I am no match for you, Doctor. Those little pawns of yours have baffled all my knights and bishops. It is a new game to me.

Frank. And to the world, lady.

Mrs H. I'll try what a spirited attack will do. There!

Frank. Not a bad move, but too late; your king's in danger.

Mrs. H. Again, Doctor.

Frank. In self-defence, madam, I must protect my poor pawns, else those knights will tread them down.

Mrs. H. Those very knights must help me, since you are for war.

Frank. You've overlooked the insignificant pawn once more; and see, he takes your castle and check-mates your king.

Mrs. H. [*Throws down pieces.*] I see, Mr. Franklin, you don't understand *our* game.

Frank. [*Rising.*] Yes, madam, I *do* understand it, and but too well It was a cunning scheme, and only to be met by cunning. I saw their lordships retire, and *know* the friendly *surprise* they intend for me. Be so good as to inform them, that I have just now learnt, their emissaries have begun to burn our towns, and murder our people. Tell them to look upon their hands, and find them stained with the blood of their relatives. If justice be not quickly done, from henceforth we are enemies. Tell them, also, that if they wish for this old useless head, I cannot spare it yet. In five minutes I shall be on my way to Paris. Farewell, madam, and learn to guard your king from treasonable pawns!

[*Exit*, C. D.

Mrs. H Farewell, Doctor; no one can be your enemy long. His ardor and persuasive eloquence have nearly shaken my loyalty. At all events, he shall not be harmed through my instrumentality.

Enter STORMONT.

Stor. Well, my dear friend, how have you succeeded?

Mrs. H. But indifferently, my lord.

Stor. Have you any useful information from him? Of course, you know war is declared?

Mrs. H. Yes, he told me so himself; and with a look of triumphant enthusiasm which was very infectious, I assure you.

Stor. He must be secured. Where is he gone to?

Mrs. H. To Paris.

Stor. Confusion! escaped?

Mrs. H. Ha! ha! It is pardonable to laugh at a baffled politician.

TABLEAU.—END OF ACT IV.

ACT V.

SCENE I.—*Handsome Interior.*

Enter FRANKLIN, *reading Card.*

"Le Chevalier Pierre Auguste Montmorenci de Pappillotte." What an astounding name! Show in the illustrious possessor of so many syllables.

Enter PAPILLOTTE.—*He is dressed superbly, and carries a muff.—Very ceremonious.*

Frank. Pray Chevalier De—whatever your name is—to what am I indebted for the honor of this visit?

Pap. Monsieur, je suis le Peruquier du Roi. I make de vig. You sent for propere one; pour votre presentation a la cour. I am come viz him.

Frank. Ah! I beg ten million of pardons, chevalier; but who, amidst such perfumery and aristocratic associations, could pick out the barber? I suppose I shall have to hide my head in one of your enormities, or etiquette will be startled from its frigid dignity. Allons, Monsieur Pappillotte.

Pap Entrez Muley et compagnon avec la peruque pour Monsieur le Philosophe—vite, vite.

Enter four black supers, dressed in oriental style, with wig boxes.

Pap. Ouvré, vite. [*Box open.*] Ah! magnifique, c'est un chef d'ouvre; do your tete de honneur to try him upon?

Frank. Too small; too small.

Pap. Pardon, monsieur, it not de peruque too small, but de head is too large. un autre. [*Box opened.*] Dere. ah Mon Dieu, c'est admirable! It is peruque pour un ange. Ciel! you know not yourself—le mirrior, monsieur—regardez!

Frank. I don't like it.

Pap. Incroyable! barbare! Vous n'avez pas bon gout, monsieur. Mais, n'importe [*Other wig shown—a black one.*] Ah! regardez la; tres distingue et tres philosophique, la magnifique peruque noire, un invention a moi meme. Voila! c'est superb; vous ete une Minerve en culotte—weesdom in de breeches, by gar!

Frank. Pshaw! I'm too old for a mountebank.

Pap. Sacre diable! c'est un imbecile, un sauvage, look den at dis, la voila!

Frank. Why you don't suppose I'm going to hide my head in that wigwam of hair!

Pap. Ah, monsieur! c'est la peruque par excellence, le nec plus ultra de la dernier mode.

Frank. I don't care what it is; I am old enough to have my own way; sense enough, I trust, to know that way is right: and courage enough to follow it, even against the ironical assaults of fashion. Do me the favor, chevalier, to take your fashionable heads away, and leave mine to nature, who, without any disparagement to your noble ancestors, I consider to be the best wig maker of the two.

Pap. Bon jour, monsieur philosophe; you have a very big head, but by gar, you have no more brain as a vig block. Allons! Sang de mon ancestre. Sare, be dam, dere is several time too moche of de philosophe, mais dere is but one perruquiere. [*Exit, followed by attendants.*

Enter SERVANT, L. H.

Serv. Here is a tailor, with your court suit.

Frank. Show him in. Another effort, I suppose, to turn Heaven's handy-work into a spectacle for fools.

(L.) *Enter* SERVANT *and* TAILOR, *with superb coat—they put it on* FRANKLIN.

Tail. Ah! superbe; fine, deliceuse; too much.

Frank. You're right, friend, a great deal too much. This coat is too courtier-like for me. Its gold embroidery is dazzling enough, but its weight makes me bow my head, against my will. Take it away; I'll wear none of your gewgaws; in my plain republican dress will I appear. If it cannot provoke envy, by its richness, it must at least command respect, for its simplicity.

SCENE II.—*The Court of the French King. All possible and conceivable magnificence.*—COURTIERS *and splendidly-dressed* LADIES *promenading.—Musicians in Gallery.—Doors thrown open. After a short pause,*

Enter VILLEROI, *Grand Chamberlain.*

Vil. The King!

[*The Music strikes up the French National Loyal Air.* "Vive Henri Quatre." *The* KING *bows to each side; ascends his Throne.*—LADIES *presented, with all the forms of a Court Presentation.—Voices heard outside, at intervals, announcing—*

"Le Viscompte De Lauzun:"
"La Marchionoise De Mauprat;"
"Le Mareschal Desmoulins;"
"Dr. Franklin." [*The* KING *rises, and meets* FRANKLIN *half-way.*

Louis. Royalty loses no respect, in paying homage to superior wisdom. Your hand, Mr. Franklin.

Frank. Your Majesty honors me over much. I did hope to have had a *private* interview with your Majesty. [KING *starts.*] I must be pardoned, if I entrench on etiquette, the religion of courts, but I was educated in the school of common sense, and am too old to learn duplicity.

Louis. Mr. Franklin, it is as new to me as it is pleasing, to be addressed as a sensible man: so accustomed am I to the tortuous finesse of a courtier's life, and the necessity of trying to unravel motives, from speeches meant to deceive, that this honesty of purpose and plain truth seems to relieve me of a painful task. Would that my ministers could profit by the lesson.

Frank. Your Majesty will grant me an interview?

Louis. Certainly, Mr. Franklin, at any other time.

Frank. Aye; but I want it now. A word of thine would send this crowd of foplings to glitter as so many suns, in little systems of their own,—here they are nebulæ: be pleased to speak it.

Louis. It is a monstrous breach of etiquette, Mr. Franklin, and for which my Grand Chamberlain will rate me soundly.

Frank. The destiny of a great people, perhaps, hangs on the few hours thus devoted to frivolity.

Louis. You shall have your wish. Villeroi!

[*Chamberlain approaches*—KING *whispers.*

Vil. So soon, sire? It is impossible!

Louis. I command it.

Vil. Your Majesty is obeyed [*Goes to each—all quietly retire.*

Frank That one man should have the power to bend so many backs. See, the circus is outdone. A court's the school to cultivate the art of posturing, and manufacture suppleness of joint.

Louis. Now, Mr. Franklin, we are alone.

Frank. That is to say, as much alone as kings can be—yon chamberlain!

Louis. Has no ears for anything that's spoken here; were one simple word to be repeated, he would soon have none at all.

Frank. Oh! the zealous devotion of fear—but to the point: it is in your majesty's power to curb the pride of your old hereditary foe.

Louis. By what means?

Frank. By wresting from its oppressive grasp a people panting to be free. It is not that they are unable to achieve their own liberty, but they would fain have the sanction of a great and wise monarch. Has your majesty perused my communication to your ministers?

Louis. I have.

Frank. And made a decision?

Louis. Fully, sir; but pardon me, the matter is too world widely important to be disposed of without proper form. Villeroi, a court! [*All enter, the King is ceremoniously enthroned.*] My lords and gentlemen, I have called you together to witness a treaty of alliance and amity between the United States of America and the kingdom of France, represented in our person, a treaty which I trust will be the means of hastening the glorious end for which those noble hearts are now contending, and place in its proper position a great and rapidly increasing country.

Frank. Let me but live to carry back with me this guarantee of my beloved country's independence, and then my earthly mission will be at an end.

Louis Mr. Franklin, it is your own treaty, sign. [*They sign treaty.*

Frank It is accomplished: this auspicious hour beholds the inauguration of a mighty principle. It is the birth-day of a giant—the small cloud, no bigger than a man's hand, that gives assurance of hereafter plenty, appears upon the fiery horizon. Let the earth rejoice, the panting toiler rain down tears of thankfulness. Upon this eventful day, the great American Republic takes its proud place upon the universal roll. May HE who rules the destinies of nations, perpetuate its unity, sanctify its usefulness, and make it the glory and the wonder of succeeding ages.

Louis. Your voices, gentlemen. Long live the Confederation of the United States.

A burst of Music—Tableau—All cheer.

CURTAIN.

A Glorious Change.

Medical treatment has been revolutionized. The Drastic purgatives with which it was the fashion to scour the system for every ailment, twenty years ago, have been abandoned. At last the discovery has been made that RENOVATION, NOT PROSTRATION, IS THE TRUE MEDICAL PHILOSOPHY. The introduction of *PLANTATION BITTERS* opened the eyes of the world to this great fact. The life-sustaining principle embodied in this great Vegetable Restorative is manifested in the weak and desponding by an immediate and most encouraging change. A pleasant glow, the precursor of returning health, is diffused through the system, and every day the invalid is conscious of a new accession of vital power. If the appetite has failed, it is quickened; if digestion has been painful and imperfect, it becomes easy and thorough; if the liver is torpid, it is roused and regulated; if the nerves are relaxed, they are strengthened and restrung; if the brain has been haunted by morbid fancies, they are put to flight, and hope and cheerfulness return. The old practice was to convulse, and rack, and strain the feeble patient with powerful cathartics. It was like clubbing a man after he was down. Happily, this false and fatal mode of treatment no longer finds favor with the enlightened members of the faculty. In the face of the extraordinary cures of general debility, dyspepsia, biliousness, constipation and mental despondency, wrought by Plantation Bitters, no practitioner, not in league with death and the undertaker, could persist in it. The terrible evacuents which were once prescribed as Spring and Summer Medicines, have utterly lost their *prestige.* The sick will not take them—and Plantation Bitters, in which are combined the elements of a stomachic, an invigorant, a mild laxative, a nervine, and an anti-bilious specific, reigns in their stead. Plantation Bitters are sold by all respectable Druggists in the United States.

THE NEW FOOD.

Office of the RAND SEA MOSS FARINE CO.,
No. 53 PARK PLACE.

In order that the public may be as fully informed as possible, in regard to the Sea Moss Farine, we submit as much information of its worth and merit as space will admit. It is exceedingly gratifying to the Company to know that their efforts to place a really good article of food in the market is so fully appreciated ; and we trust that in the future, as well as in the past, we may continue to merit the appreciation of all.

[*From the Weekly Tribune of Dec.* 15, 1869.]

AMERICAN INSTITUTE FARMERS' CLUB,

Session of December 7, 1869, held at Cooper Union. Alderman Nathan C. Ely in the chair, John W. Chambers, Secretary. The first subject introduced was—

"A NEW ARTICLE OF FOOD."

The "ex-Mayor of Boston," Hon. J. V. C. Smith, M. D., distributed some parcels of SEA MOSS FARINE, which he said is offered to the public as the most nutritive, delicious and cheap article of its class ever manufactured in this country or in Europe. The ex-Mayor gave a lengthened professional evidence in favor of the preparation, and detailed like opinions of medical gentlemen in Europe.

To ascertain if these claims are well founded, the following ladies—who are distinguished for their intelligence and social position, and as acting under the authority of the Institute—were appointed a Committee to examine it and report : Mrs. L. E. Lyman, Mrs. J. W. Chambers, Mrs. D. T. Conner, Mrs. D. B. Bruen and Mrs. M. J. Cushing, M. D.

[*From the Weekly Tribune, Dec.* 22, 1869.]

AMERICAN INSTITUTE FARMERS' CLUB,

Session of Tuesday, Dec. 21, 1869, held at Cooper Union. Nathan C. Ely, Chairman ; John W. Chambers, Secretary.

Report on the New Article of Food—Sea Moss Farine.

The Committee of Ladies, Mrs. Lyman, Mrs. Chambers and others, requested to report on Carrageen, or Irish Moss (from which SEA MOSS FARINE is manufactured), as a dish for the table, finds that the substance grows on rocks and stones on the sea-coasts of Europe, and in peculiar abundance on the Atlantic coast of Ireland, where it is chiefly gathered. It is said to be a native of the United States, and is found in limited quantities on the coast of Massachusetts. It is picked from the rocks at low tide. After being washed, it is dried in the sun. Chemists and doctors who have analyzed it, find it is nutritive and demulcent; and, being easy of digestion, it forms a useful article of diet as a substitute for grain foods, and is particularly recommended in chronic pectoral affections, scrofulous complaints, dysentery, diarrhea, &c. Carrageen is very gelatinous, and very valuable as food. It is recognized as superior to all orders of moss as demulcent, and in its nutritive qualities. It is said that Napoleon Bonaparte said to Dr. O'Meara, at St. Helena, that it was employed as an article of diet by physicians in Corsica, in the treatment of tumors and cancers, on account of the iodine it contains. It is used in England and France as a light and nourishing article of food.

A NEW FOOD SOURCE.

The moss, as it comes from the sea, is filled with sand, pebbles, small shells, &c., and very saline in taste: and, prepared as food in its original state, is very troublesome to the housekeeper, while it is very easy to prepare when made from SEA MOSS FARINE. By this process, it is first thoroughly washed and deprived of its extreme saline taste. It is then picked over by hand and desiccated, after which it passes through several mills and machines, by which it is cleaned perfectly, and reduced to a powdered and concentrated condition without being deprived of its refreshing ocean flavor. A packet of Corn Starch, Maizena or Farina costs 16c. at retail, and makes, combined with milk, without eggs, only from four to six quarts of Blanc Mange Pudding, while SEA MOSS FARINE, costing 25c., will produce full sixteen quarts. The Committee are satisfied that as a cheap, simple and ready dessert, or a dish for young children and for invalids, it will be found, *as thus prepared*, a valuable addition to articles more generally known and widely used.

(Signed,)

MRS. L. E. LYMAN, (wife of the Agricultural Editor of the N. Y. Tribune.
MRS. J. W. CHAMBERS, (wife of the Secretary of the American Institute.)
MRS. D. T. CONNER, 5-Mile Run, N. J.
MRS. D. B. BRUEN, Newark, N. J.
MRS. MARIA J. CUSHING, M. D., 231 East 40th St., N. Y.

ASTOR HOUSE, NEW YORK, Jan., 1870.

RAND SEA MOSS FARINE CO.:

Gentlemen: We commenced the use of your Sea Moss Farine at your earnest solicitation, but very reluctantly, and without any faith in it, from the fact that so many new articles of food are daily offered, and prove, in almost every case, to be utterly worthless. We are very happy to say that yours has not only proved an exception, but is a *decided success*. It not only possesses *real merit*, but makes a *delicious dessert*. We shall continue to use it for two reasons: *first*, the guests of the Astor House like it; and *second*, *we* like it, because it is *by far the cheapest article in the market* for Blanc Mange, Puddings, Creams, &c.

Very respectfully yours,
C. A. STETSON'S SONS

BROOKLYN, N. Y., Sept. 13, 1869.

My Dear Rand: I have submitted your "Sea Moss Farine" to the "kitchen cabinet," and the decision is decidedly favorable. It quite surpassed my most sanguine expectations. There is a slight and yet positive sea flavor—just a hint of the ocean—in it, which is rare and delightful. My wife liked it, the children liked it—took to it naturally—and all at the table passed up their dishes twice. The peoples' proverb was verified, that "*the proof of a pudding is in eating it.*"

Your friend and brother,
J. HYATT SMITH,
Pastor of the Lee Ave. Baptist Church.

PARKER HOUSE, BOSTON, Jan. 25, 1870.

RAND SEA MOSS FARINE CO., New York:

We are using "Sea Moss Farine," and find it just what you state it is—real, pure Irish Moss, so refined, desiccated and condensed that we can prepare dishes for dessert from it in a few minutes, instead of hours, when made from the crude moss.

We very cordially recommend it (as prepared by you) far superior and much cheaper than Corn Starch, Maizena, Farina, Gelatine, or any like article for Blanc Mange, Creams, Puddings, Charlotte Russe, &c., &c. We hope that its delicate and elegant appearance on the table—and more than all this, its well-known healthfulness and delicious flavor—will command for it millions of consumers.

Respectfully yours,
H. D. PARKER & CO.

A NEW FOOD SOURCE.

We have received the following characteristic note from the celebrated Dio Lewis, A. M., M. D., Principal of the Lexington Young Ladies' Seminary for Physical Education, author of "Weak Lungs, and How to Make Them Strong," of "The New Gymnastics for Men, Women and Children," and "Lecture on Physical Culture:"

17 Beacon Street, Boston, January 25, 1870.

RAND SEA MOSS FARINE Co.:

My wife says that your new preparation, "Sea Moss Farine," is *worth its weight in* GOLD; *no trouble, so sure,* and so *delicious.*

Believe me, in addition to my "better half's" testimony, when I add that my *most toothsome tooth* is very thankfully yours. DIO LEWIS.

FROM THE PRESS.

No such sensation has been created in the food market during the present century, as that occasioned by the introduction of the *new staff of life,* known as Sea Moss Farine. It is difficult to tell the truth about this extraordinary article of diet without being suspected of exaggeration.—*Boston Post.*

A still greater number of distinguished physicians and scientific chemists indorse it as a nutritient of the very first class, while every housekeeper who uses it admits that it is fully fifty per cent. cheaper than Maizena, Farina, Corn Starch, or any other kindred preparation.—*Boston Times.*

Housekeepers declare that the quantity of exquisite Custards, Blanc Mange, Light Pudding, Creams, Jelly, &c., producible from the Farine, exceeds by one half that obtainable from any other glutinous agent used in cooking.—*St. Louis Republican.*

One experiment will convince the most skeptical that with Sea Moss Farine they can produce unequalled Custards, Puddings, Jellies, Charlotte Russe, Creams, Soups, &c., &c.—*Express.*

Here, then, we have an entirely new article of food of the most delicate and inviting character, adapted to the use of the table for Blanc Mange, Puddings, Charlotte de Russe, &c., and almost invaluable for use by the invalid. It is simple, delicate, nutritious, harmless, remedial and economical, as it can be furnished for one-third to one-half the cost of Corn Starch, Maizena, Farina, &c., for all of which it is more than a substitute. It is made up without trouble, and will always be good. Try it; and our word for it, you will continue in its use.—*Independent.*

The Company state at least fifty delicious dishes can be made from the Sea Moss Farine, and give in their circular the recipes for many of them. We consider Mr. Rand's discovery a highly-important one for the millions, and indeed for all classes of society, in these stringent times.—*The Weekly.*

It has been placed, so to speak, in the front rank of our food staples, and all that has been said of it by the patentee (Mr. Rand), and the Company interested in its sale, appears to be approved and confirmed by public opinion.—*The Mail.*

As to its deliciousness, the "proof of the pudding is in eating it;" and we feel confident that no man or woman who has once eaten of a Blanc Mange, Pudding, Custard, Cream, Charlotte Russe, or any other delicacy prepared with this marine Godsend, will deny its claim to rank among the table luxuries of the period.—*Tribune.*

This apparently impossibility has been overcome—experimental science overcomes almost every obstacle, now-a-days—and Irish Moss, purified, concentrated, and rendered an absolute luxury, as SEA MOSS FARINE, will hereafter be quoted as a food staple in the markets of the world.—*The World.*

Hence it will be cheap as long as the sea and rocks last—which will be long enough for all practicable purposes. Our main object in this article has been to place what we believe to be a subject of great importance, in its true light; nothing more, nothing less.—*Home Journal.*

www.ingramcontent.com/pod-product-compliance
Lightning Source LLC
LaVergne TN
LVHW011132110826
845150LV00008B/2298
* 9 7 8 1 4 1 8 1 9 4 1 4 7 *